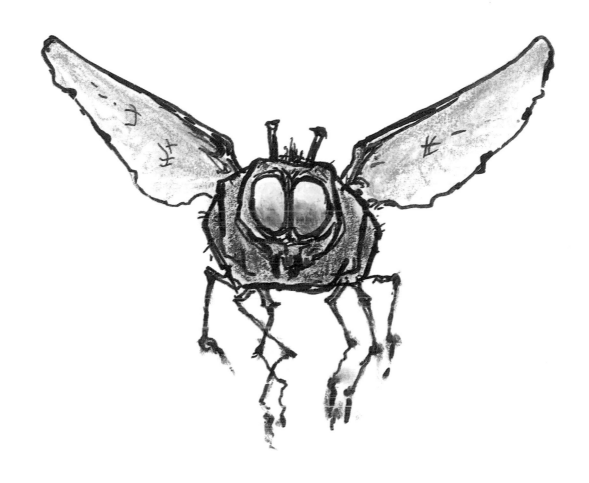

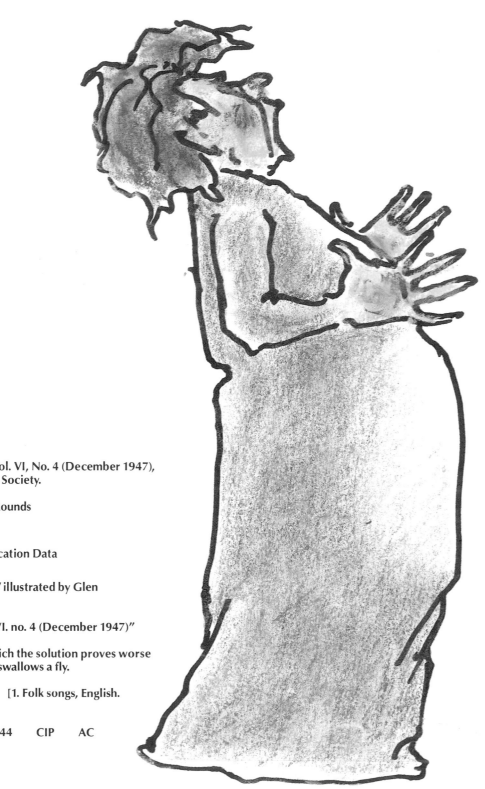

Text reprinted from *Hoosier Folklore,* Vol. VI, No. 4 (December 1947), with permission of the Hoosier Folklore Society.

Illustrations copyright © 1990 by Glen Rounds
Printed in the United States of America

Library of Congress Cataloging-in-Publication Data

Rounds, Glen
I know an old lady who swallowed a fly / illustrated by Glen Rounds.—1st ed.
p.   cm.
"Reprinted from Hoosier folklore, vol. VI. no. 4 (December 1947)"
—T.p. verso.
Summary: A cumulative folk song in which the solution proves worse than the predicament when an old lady swallows a fly.
ISBN 0-8234-0814-0
1. Folk-songs, English—England—Texts.   [1. Folk songs, English.
2. Nonsense verses.]   I. Title.
PZ8.3.R78laf   1990
782.42162'21'00268—dc20   89-46244   CIP   AC
ISBN 0-8234-0814-0
ISBN 0-8234-0908-2 (pbk.)

I KNOW AN OLD LADY WHO SWALLOWED A FLY

illustrations by

GLEN ROUNDS

Holiday House/New York

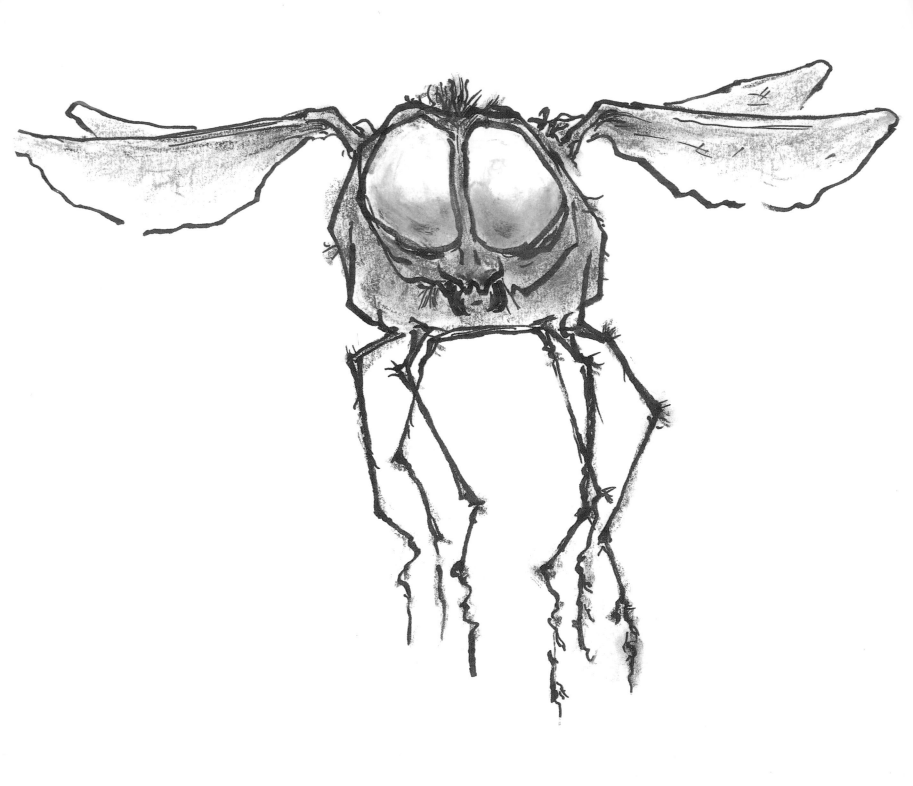

I know an old lady who
swallowed a fly.

I don't know WHY she
swallowed the fly.

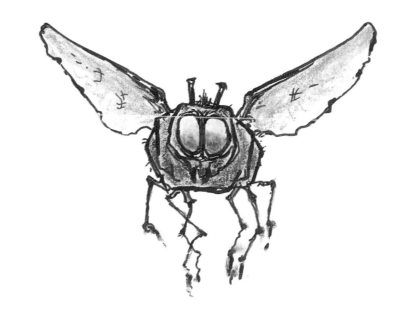

Poor old lady!
I guess she'll die.

I know an old lady who
swallowed a spider.
It wrickled and ickled and
tickled inside her.

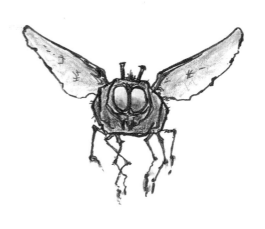

She swallowed the spider
to catch the fly.
I don't know WHY she
swallowed the fly.

Poor old lady!
I guess she'll die.

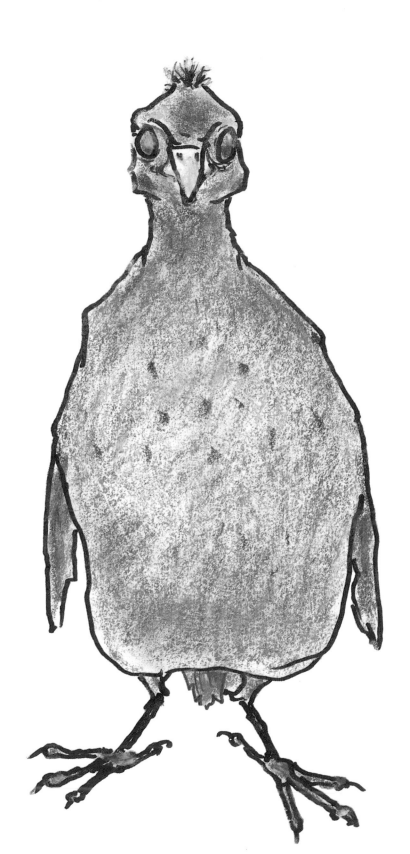

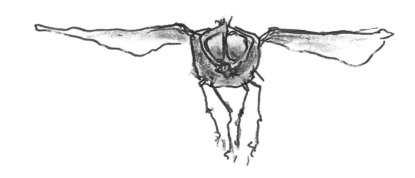

I know an old lady who
      swallowed a bird.
She swallowed a bird?
      My, how absurd!

She swallowed the bird
      to catch the spider.
It wrickled and ickled and
      tickled inside her.

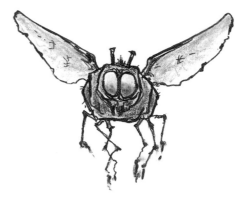

She swallowed the spider
    to catch the fly.
I don't know WHY she
    swallowed the fly.

Poor old lady!
I guess she'll die.

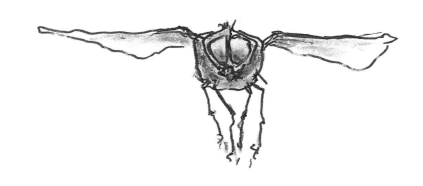

I know an old lady who
            swallowed a cat.
She swallowed a cat?
            Imagine that!

She swallowed the cat
            to catch the bird.
She swallowed a bird?
            My, how absurd!

She swallowed the bird
to catch the spider.
It wrickled and ickled and
tickled inside her.

She swallowed the spider
to catch the fly.
I don't know WHY she
swallowed the fly.

Poor old lady!
I guess she'll die.

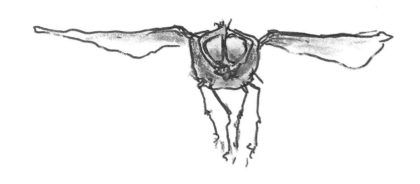

I know an old lady who
        swallowed a dog.
She swallowed a dog?
        My, what a hog!

She swallowed the dog
        to catch the cat.
She swallowed a cat?
        Imagine that!

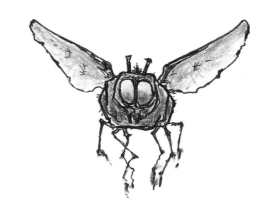

She swallowed the cat
to catch the bird.
She swallowed a bird?
My, how absurd!

She swallowed the bird
to catch the spider.
It wrickled and ickled and
tickled inside her.

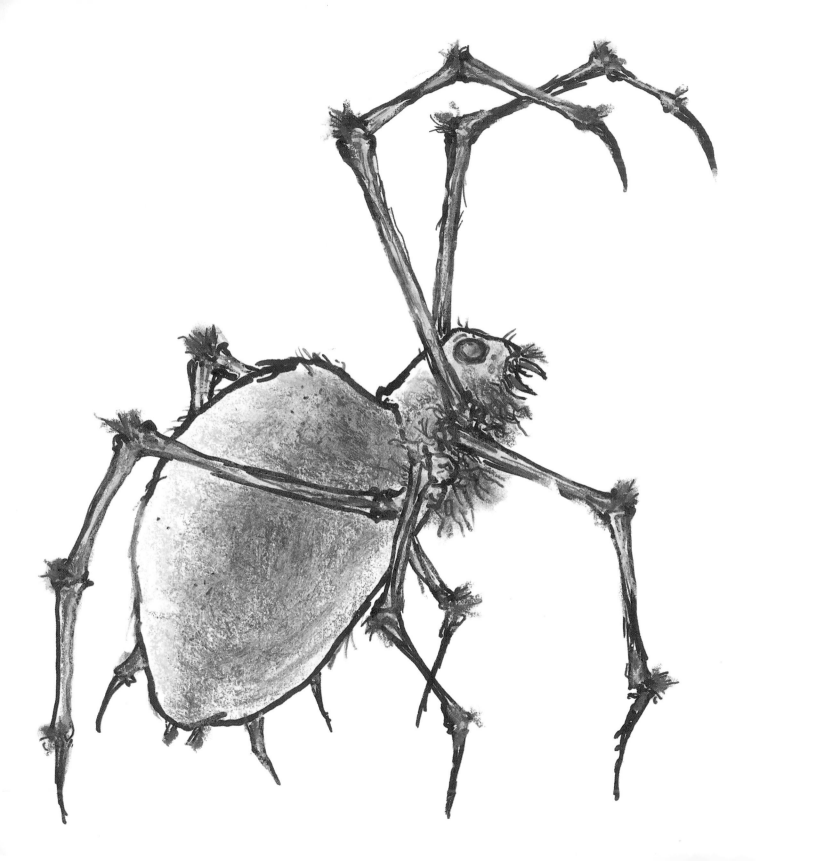

She swallowed the spider
to catch the fly.
I don't know WHY she
swallowed the fly.

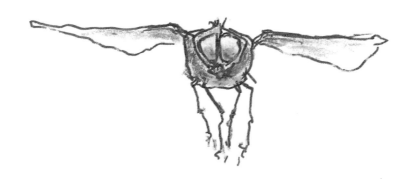

Poor old lady!
I guess she'll die.

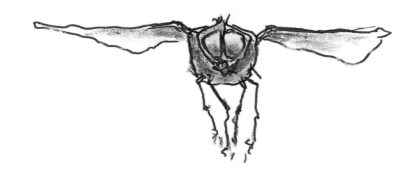

I know an old lady who
            swallowed a goat.
She swallowed a goat—it got
            stuck in her throat.

She swallowed the goat
            to catch the dog.
She swallowed a dog?
            My, what a hog!

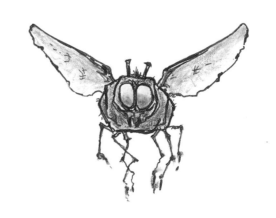

She swallowed the dog
       to catch the cat.
She swallowed a cat?
       Imagine that!

She swallowed the cat
       to catch the bird.
She swallowed a bird?
       My, how absurd!

She swallowed the bird
      to catch the spider.
It wrickled and ickled and
      tickled inside her.

She swallowed the spider
      to catch the fly.
I don't know WHY she
      swallowed the fly.

Poor old lady!
I guess she'll die.

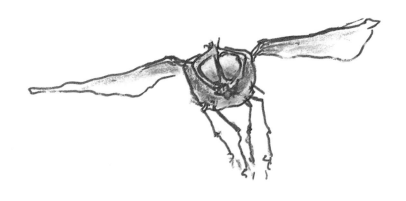

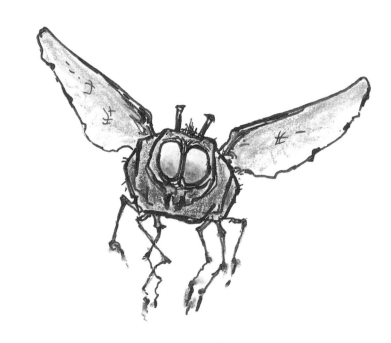

I know an
old lady who
swallowed a
horse.

Poor old lady!
She died, of course.